A FUNNY THING HAPPENED ON THE WAY TO THE FORUM

A FUNNY THING HAPPENED

ON THE WAY TO THE FORUM

THE WORLD'S OLDEST JOKE BOOK

TRANSLATED BY DAN CROMPTON

Michael O'Mara Books Limited

First published in Great Britain in 2010 by
Michael O'Mara Books Limited
9 Lion Yard
Tremadoc Road
London SW4 7NQ

Papers used by Michael O'Mara Books Limited are natural, recyclable
products made from wood grown in sustainable forests. The manufacturing
processes conform to the environmental regulations of the country of origin.

A CIP catalogue record for this book is available from the British Library.

ISBN: 978-1-84317-498-1

1 3 5 7 9 10 8 6 4 2

www.mombooks.com

Jacket design by mint julep
Text design and typesetting by www.envydesign.co.uk
Illustrations by mint julep

Printed and bound in Great Britain by Clays Ltd, St Ives plc

CONTENTS

CONTENTS

ACKNOWLEDGEMENTS

This book would not have come about at all – let alone come about looking as lovely as it does – without the imagination and enthusiasm of my editor Silvia Crompton and publicist Ana McLaughlin at Michael O'Mara Books, and of the illustrator Rachael Ludbrook and the designers at Envy. Thanks also to Guy for not allowing my sense of humour to become any more sophisticated than a schoolboy's.

Finally, a quick apology to my former Greek tutors, who presumably fell off their chairs when they saw my name on a book. It would appear that I *was* listening.

INTRODUCTION

I t turns out that farting has been funny for a very, very
long time.

Well, at least since the fourth century AD, which is
when the Roman joke book *Philogelos* (often translated
as *The Laughter-Lover*, although *The Joker* probably makes
more sense) was put together.

We don't know much about the Greek authors, Hierocles
and Philagrios. Greece was part of the Roman Empire
by this stage, which is why there are a few references to
Rome (and a Rome-related title). But our two authors
are unmistakably Greek, and while I like to think of them
writing this collection of jokes during an increasingly

boozy evening at the local taverna – it would certainly account for some of the clangers – in truth they may never have known each other, nor even existed. We don't even know whether the collection was written down in one sitting or passed down verbally through generations, with new authors adding their own favourite one-liners along the way. What we *do* know is that it is the oldest surviving collection of jokes in the world. And that people in the fourth century found nothing funnier than a eunuch with a hernia.

The Romans had done most of their marching, pillaging and road-building by the fourth century. The people we think about when we think about the Romans (Julius Caesar, Virgil, that bloke from *Gladiator*) were all long gone, and the Roman Empire now covered such a huge proportion of the known world that it became difficult to manage. Civil wars were breaking out all over the place between military rulers, and it was almost time for the Romans to call it a day.

Fortunately, Hierocles and Philagrios seem to have been

completely oblivious to the end-of-an-era hullaballoo going on around them, and preferred instead to spend their days joking about nagging wives and bad breath.

Their sense of humour differs from how we joke today: the Greek language was very precise and taken very literally, so any play on words or deviation from logical common sense – the sort of scenario that would make us think, 'yes, how silly' – had the Greeks rolling around in stitches. Absurd situations, foolishness and confusions of identity form the basis of most of these jokes, alongside regional stereotypes and the outrageous stupidity of all foreigners. While some of the jokes are just as funny today as they were 1,600 years ago, others have not withstood the test of time quite so well. We can still chuckle at classic comic laughing stocks such as the idiot (he bought one thirty-year-old slave instead of two nubile fifteen-year-olds) or the misogynist (his wife said she'd hang herself if he died – 'Do it while I'm still alive, darling.'), and be surprised to see just how ancient the old chestnut about talkative hairdressers is ('How shall I cut your hair, sir?' 'In silence.'), but the coward (punchline: he was a total wimp) and the greedy man (punchline: he was terribly greedy) don't quite stand up to the wit on which we pride ourselves today.

But who cares if some of the things that amused Hierocles and his pal in the fourth century aren't quite the same things that make us laugh in the twenty-first? The fact that these jokes have survived for 1,600 years surely gives them a right to an airing – and you'll soon find that even the very worst of the bunch are so bad it's funny.

TRANSLATOR'S NOTE

There have been a handful of academic translations of *Philogelos* in recent centuries, full of footnotes (mainly in Latin) and immaculately researched scholarly wrangling over what most of us would consider minor historical or linguistic points. If that's the sort of translation you're after, there's a 'further reading' list at the back of this book.

My job in producing the first commercial publication of the collection is to ignore all of that and simply make the jokes funny to a modern, non-academic audience. I've avoided old-fashioned expressions if they can be rendered more amusing by modern vocabulary, and I haven't included the dozen or so jokes that simply don't work in any language other than Ancient Greek. Adding credibility to my theory that the jokes were written during a drunken night down the taverna, there are numerous examples of near-word-for-word repetition, which I have also cut out.

What we're left with is approximately 240 smart-arsed quips and puerile one-liners that prove beyond doubt that, when it comes to witty repartee, humankind will never be able to top 'Yeah? Well, you smell.'

IDIOTS

An idiot asks a silversmith to make him a lamp.

'How big do you want me to make it?' the silversmith asks.

'Big enough for eight people to see by.'

Did you hear the one about the idiot who nearly drowned? He vowed he'd never go into the water again until he had learnt to swim.

An idiot goes to the doctor and says, 'Doctor, doctor –
when I wake up in the morning, I'm dizzy for half an
hour, but then it clears up again.'

'So get up half an hour later,' the doctor replies.

An idiot is selling his horse. A potential buyer, curious
about the horse's age, asks whether it has lost its first set
of teeth yet.

'Oh, it's lost its second set already,' boasts the idiot.
'First it knocked out mine, and then it knocked out
my father's.'

A man bumps into an idiot and says, 'Ah, my quick-witted
friend – I had a dream that I was talking to you.'

'Oh dear,' replies the idiot, 'I must have been too busy
to listen.'

An idiot sees his local doctor walking towards him, and quickly hides his face. His friend asks him what's up.

'It's so long since I was last ill,' explains the idiot, 'that I'm embarrassed to see him.'

An idiot has his tonsils removed and the doctor tells him not to speak, so he gets his slave to return the greetings of anyone he encounters.

'Don't think it rude that my slave is returning my greetings,' he interrupts whenever his slave starts talking. 'My doctor ordered me not to speak.'

An idiot was trying to catch a mouse that had been nibbling through his books, so he sat still all night with a piece of meat in his mouth.

AN IDIOT WANTS TO TEACH HIS
MULE NOT TO EAT TOO MUCH,
SO DOESN'T GIVE HIM ANY FOOD.
THE MULE DIES OF HUNGER.

'WHAT AN OUTRAGE!' EXCLAIMS
THE IDIOT. 'AS SOON AS HE'S
LEARNT NOT TO EAT, HE GOES
AND DIES ON ME!'

Did you hear the one about the idiot who wanted to see what he looked like when he was sleeping? He looked at his reflection and closed his eyes.

Two idiots are complaining that their fathers are still alive.

'I've got it,' says the first idiot, 'Why don't we just strangle our own fathers?'

'No way!' says the second. 'We don't want people to call us patricides! But, if you like, you can kill mine and I'll kill yours.'

An idiot has a dream that he has trodden on a nail, so wakes up and bandages his foot. When his friend finds out what he's doing, he says, 'We're such morons – I can't believe you've been sleeping barefoot.'

An idiot is selling his horse, and someone asks him if it has ever shown signs of being nervous.

'By god, no!' says the idiot. 'It's never been out of its stable long enough to get nervous.'

An idiot has bought a house, and he sticks his head out of the window to ask the neighbours if it suits him.

An idiot spends days looking for a book he's lost, but doesn't find it. Then one day, as he's eating lettuce, he suddenly spots the book lying in the corner of the room. The next day, he bumps into a friend who is mourning the loss of some items of clothing.

'Don't worry,' says the idiot. 'Just buy some lettuce and eat it while looking into the corner of the room. You'll find your clothes in no time.'

AN IDIOT IS GOING INTO TOWN
AND HIS FRIEND ASKS, 'COULD
YOU BRING ME BACK TWO
FIFTEEN-YEAR-OLD SLAVES?'

'SURE,' REPLIES THE IDIOT. 'AND
IF I CAN'T FIND TWO OF THEM,
I'LL GET YOU ONE
THIRTY-YEAR-OLD INSTEAD.'

A friend of this idiot is abroad, and writes to him asking to be sent some books. The idiot completely ignores the letter. Once the friend has returned, the idiot bumps into him.

'Oh! That letter you sent me about the books ...' he stammers. 'I never got it.'

Disgruntled customer: That slave you sold me has only gone and died!
Idiot: By god, he never did anything of the sort when I owned him.

After a dinner, two idiots each keep trying to escort the other to his home out of politeness, so neither of them gets anywhere.

An idiot wants to go to sleep, but doesn't have a pillow, so he orders his slave to put a pot under his head.

'But it'll be too hard,' the slave points out.

'Well, fill it with feathers, then,' snaps the idiot.

An idiot bumps into a friend and says, 'I heard you had died!'

'Well, as you can see,' replies the friend, 'I'm quite alive.'

'But the guy who told me is so much more trustworthy than you.'

An idiot goes into the bathhouse as soon as it opens, and there's not a single person inside. He turns to his slave and says, 'It looks to me as though the water isn't washing properly.'

DID YOU HEAR THE ONE ABOUT
THE IDIOT WHO WANTED TO
CATCH A SPARROW? HE LAID OUT
HIS CLOAK UNDER A TREE, AND
SHOOK THE BRANCHES.

An idiot is fighting with his father.

'You bastard!' he cries. 'You don't see how much you've made me suffer! If you'd never been born, I would have inherited my grandfather's good character.'

A sick idiot agrees to pay his doctor's full fee, but only if his treatment works. Later, the man's wife has a go at him for drinking wine while he's unwell.

'What?' replies the idiot. 'Do you want me to be cured and have to pay the doctor?'

A dog bites an idiot's thumb.

'Thank god it didn't get my cloak and tear it,' says the idiot.

One of two twin brothers dies, and an idiot goes up
to the living one and asks, 'Was it you who died,
or your brother?'

An idiot is about to set sail, so he sends for his tablets in
order to write his will. Fearful of being shipwrecked, his
slaves start wailing.

'Calm down!' snaps the idiot. 'If I drown, I'm setting
you all free.'

An idiot on a horse is crossing a river by boat, but
doesn't get out of the saddle. When asked why he won't
dismount, he explains, 'I'm in a bit of a hurry.'

AN IDIOT GOES SAILING IN REALLY
STORMY WEATHER, AND HIS
SLAVES START SCREAMING.

'DON'T WORRY!' HE SCREAMS
BACK. 'IN MY WILL, I'VE SET
YOU ALL FREE!'

IDIOTS

An idiot is asked over for dinner, but doesn't eat a thing. One of the other guests asks him why he's not eating.

'I wouldn't want it to look as if I only came here to eat,' he replies.

An idiot's son is playing with a ball, which falls into a well. Leaning into the well, the boy sees his own reflection and asks for his ball back. When he tells his dad he can't retrieve his ball, the idiot father leans over into the well, sees his own reflection and shouts, 'Hey! Give the boy his ball back!'

An idiot goes to visit his sick friend and asks him how he's doing. When his friend is unable to answer, the idiot becomes angry and says, 'I hope I get sick soon, and then *I* won't answer *you*.'

An idiot used to go round asking everyone how much their clothes were worth. His father heard about this and had a stern word with him.

'But dad,' the idiot protested, 'you're just listening to gossip rather than the truth.'

His father named the man who had told him.

'And you believe *that* man?' snorted the idiot, 'Who won't even spend 50 drachmas on his clothes?'

An idiot is trying to sell his horse, and a man comes along and starts examining the horse's teeth.

'Why are you worrying about its teeth?' the idiot exclaims. 'If only it could walk as well as it eats!'

Did you hear the one about the idiot who bought a stolen urn? He covered it in tar so that no one would recognize it.

An idiot whose father is really ill asks his friends to buy wreaths to wear at the funeral. When the father recovers the next day, the idiot's friends are really annoyed.

'I'm so embarrassed that you've had to fork out for these wreaths,' says the idiot, 'so wear them tomorrow. I'm going to bury my dad no matter what.'

A powerful idiot's young son dies. Upon seeing so many people turning up to the funeral, he laments, 'How embarrassing that I only have one small boy to bury in front of such a big crowd.'

Two idiots are walking together when one of them has to drop back to take a leak. When he carries on walking, he finds his friend has written 'CATCH UP WITH ME' on the next milestone.

'NO,' he writes beneath it, 'YOU WAIT FOR ME.'

An idiot sleeps in the bed next to his dad's, and every night secretly stands on his bed to eat the bunch of grapes hanging above him. One night, his dad hides a lamp under the bed, and suddenly shines it on the idiot when he stands up. Still standing upright, the idiot starts snoring and pretends to be asleep.

An idiot heard that only the judgements in the afterlife are just.

Since his hearing was in court, he hanged himself.

TWO IDIOTS ARE WALKING
TOGETHER WHEN ONE OF THEM
SEES A BLACK HEN.

'LOOK,' HE SAYS TO HIS FRIEND,
'SHE MUST BE WEARING BLACK
BECAUSE HER ROOSTER IS DEAD.'

One night, an idiot jumps into his own grandmother's bed. His father discovers him, and beats him for it.

'All this time you've been mounting my mother without a single word from me,' protests the idiot, 'and now you get angry when you catch me just *once* with yours?'

An idiot's land agent comes to break the news that the river has taken his whole property.

'What a cheek!' screams the idiot.

Did you hear the one about the idiot moneylender who called in his debts? He ordered a sailor to buy him a cremation urn and two smaller urns for his eight-year-old sons, which would grow to the right size with interest.

An idiot sees a deep well in his own field and asks if the water is drinkable. His farmhand tells him that his parents used to drink from it.

'What long necks they must have had to drink from such a deep well,' says the idiot.

An idiot falls into a pit and keeps shouting out for help, but no one comes to his rescue.

'I'd be a complete fool,' he says to himself, 'if I don't beat them all when I get out for not listening to me, nor bringing me a ladder.'

An idiot sits down to dinner with his dad, and laid out before them is a huge lettuce that has lots of small sprouts growing off it. The idiot says, 'You eat the children, father, and I will eat the mother.'

AN IDIOT GOES TO HIS FIELD
AFTER SOME TIME AWAY AND
SEES HIS FLOCK GOING OUT TO
PASTURE. HEARING THEM BLEAT
AS THEY NORMALLY DO, HE ASKS
WHY THEY'RE DOING THIS. HIS
SHEPHERD JOKES THAT THEY'RE
WELCOMING HIM.

'HOW NICE OF THEM!' SAYS THE
IDIOT. 'WELL, SEEING AS I'VE HAD
SOME TIME OFF, GIVE THEM A
HOLIDAY, TOO – DON'T TAKE THEM
OUT TO PASTURE FOR THREE DAYS.'

An idiot student writes to his father from Athens, all big-headed because he's now been educated.

'I hope you get put on trial for your life,' he writes. 'Then I'll come and show you what a lawyer I've become!'

An idiot, a barber and a bald guy go walking together. When they have to set up camp in the middle of nowhere, they decide to stay up in four-hour shifts in order to watch over their belongings.

The first on guard is the barber – and, in a mischievous mood, he shaves the idiot's hair off as he's sleeping, and then wakes him up when his shift is done. The idiot jumps up and, scratching his head, feels that it's completely bald.

'What a total moron that barber is!' cries the idiot. 'Instead of waking *me* up, he's woken the bald guy.'

An idiot's dad orders him to get rid of the child he is having by a slave-girl. The idiot responds, 'You go and bury your own child before you tell me to get rid of mine!'

An idiot student completely runs out of money, so starts selling all his books. When he next writes to his father, he says, 'Congratulate me – my books are already supporting me!'

An idiot walks into a bathhouse and his slave splashes warm water on his feet.

'You idiot!' yells the idiot. 'Why on earth are you pouring warm water onto such a cold-hearted man?'

PEOPLE TELL A YOUNG IDIOT THAT HIS BEARD IS COMING, SO HE GOES TO THE FRONT GATE TO WELCOME IT. WHEN HIS FRIEND REALIZES WHAT HE'S DOING, HE SAYS, 'NO WONDER PEOPLE THINK WE'RE IDIOTS – HOW DO YOU KNOW YOUR BEARD ISN'T COMING THROUGH THE BACK GATE?'

An idiot has to walk past many milestones before he gets home – so, to make it closer, he knocks down seven of them.

Someone tells an idiot that he ate a wonderful piece of cured ham recently, so the next day the idiot goes to his butcher and asks him to slaughter a cured pig.

An idiot schoolteacher suddenly looks up and screams, 'Dionysius in the corner there – you're being disorderly!'

One of the students points out that Dionysius hasn't arrived yet.

'Well,' says the idiot, 'he'll be disorderly when he does.'

During the Millennial Games in Rome, an idiot sees a defeated athlete crying. To comfort him, he says, 'Don't worry – you'll win at the next Millennial Games.'

An idiot is accompanying a governor who is blind in his right eye. When they've been around the vineyard and observed how wonderful the grapes on one side are, the idiot says, 'When we turn around and walk back, you'll see just how lovely the grapes on the other side are, too!'

Q: What did the idiot do when he realized his trousers were too tight to get on?
A: Shaved his legs.

AN IDIOT'S SON IS SENT OFF
TO WAR BY HIS FATHER, AND
PROMISES TO RETURN WITH
THE HEAD OF ONE OF THE
ENEMY SOLDIERS. THE IDIOT TELLS
HIS SON, 'EVEN IF I SEE
YOU COMING BACK WITHOUT
A HEAD, I'LL BE GLAD.'

An idiot sees a ship in the river that is so full of grain that it's riding low in the water.

'Goodness,' he remarks, 'if the river rises by even a tiny amount, that ship will sink!'

An idiot meets his father-in-law for the first time in years, and is asked how his school friend is doing.

'Oh, he's doing really well,' replies the idiot, 'now that he's buried his wife's old man.'

An idiot is leaving a wedding.

'I wish you all the best,' he tells the couple, 'and pray that you always have weddings this good.'

An idiot writes a legal case on someone's behalf, and reads it out in public. His lawyer freaks out and says he's just given away all the secrets of the case to their opponent.

'You moron!' replies the idiot. 'I haven't told them anything important, have I?'

An idiot goes to visit the parents of a school friend who has died. Wailing with grief, the father cries, 'Child – you have finished me!'

'Child!' laments the mother, 'you have taken my whole future from me!'

'If he did all these things,' whispers the idiot, 'he should have been cremated when he was alive!'

An idiot goes to visit a really sick friend. When he arrives, the wife says, with tears in her eyes, 'Sadly ... he has already left us.'

'Oh, well,' says the idiot. 'When he comes back, tell him I dropped by.'

Did you hear the one about the idiot who received a sample cloth exactly the right size to cover his table? When he got it home, he couldn't work out which side was the length and which side the width.

The same idiot also said that Scribonia's tomb was beautiful and luxurious, but just that the location was a bit miserable.

An idiot is riding a scraggy horse, and someone says to him, 'Your horse is heading towards death, mate.'

'Great,' says the idiot. 'That's where I'm going, too.'

An idiot goes to the temple of Serapis, and the priest gives him an olive branch and prays, 'May the god be gracious to you.'

'Oh, I'm fine,' says the idiot, 'I'm a free man. Let him be gracious to my pig of a slave!'

An idiot has just had to bury his son, and meets the boy's teacher.

'I must apologise that my son didn't make it to school today,' says the idiot. 'He's dead.'

AN IDIOT IS LYING IN HIS SICK BED, AND GETS HUNGRY. HE CAN'T BELIEVE THAT THE MIDDAY BELL HASN'T BEEN RUNG YET, SO DEMANDS THAT THE SUNDIAL BE BROUGHT FOR HIM TO CHECK.

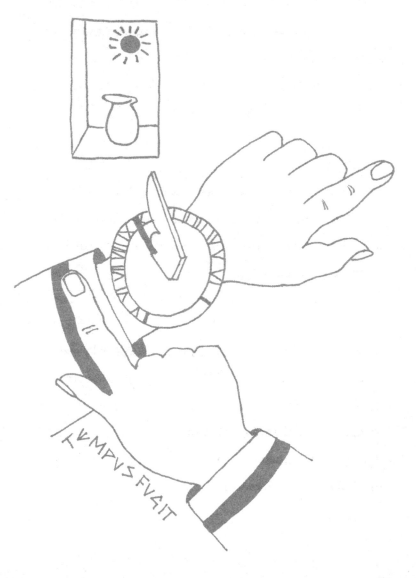

An idiot has bought some ancient paintings from Corinth, and is loading them up into a ship.

'If you lose these,' he warns the sailors, 'I will demand brand-new replacements from you.'

An idiot is out sailing when his boat is hit by a sudden storm. The other passengers start throwing all their belongings overboard to make the boat lighter. Wanting to follow suit, the idiot takes out a cheque for 1,500,000 drachmas and crosses out the 500, saying, 'Look how much lighter I've made the boat!'

An idiot is out sailing and caught in another storm, and all the other passengers start panicking.

'It's your own fault for being so stingy,' says the idiot. 'I paid an extra 10 drachmas so that I'm sailing at the captain's own risk.'

An idiot is climbing up a wall in the middle of a battle, when someone empties a chamber pot all over him.

'Hey!' he shouts up. 'This is supposed to be a clean fight!'

Did you hear about the idiot whose ship began to run aground off the River Rhine? He ran below deck and started to push against the ceiling.

AN IDIOT IS RETURNING HOME
FROM A FOREIGN TRIP, AND IS
ABSOLUTELY AMAZED TO FIND
HIMSELF CLIMBING A STEEP HILL.

'WHEN I FIRST CAME THIS WAY,'
HE SAYS TO HIMSELF, 'IT WAS A
NICE DOWNHILL STROLL. HOW
CAN IT HAVE TRANSFORMED
INTO SUCH A STEEP CLIMB
ON MY WAY BACK?'

The same idiot is addressing his troops.

'I want you to spend a lot of today sitting down,' he says, 'because tomorrow you've got a *really* long way to march.'

An idiot has just moved into a new house, and, after cleaning the area in front of the gate, he sticks up a sign: 'If You Drop Any Litter Here, You Won't Get It Back.'

An idiot has lost a one-drachma coin, and his dad is about to beat him.

'Don't get angry!' pleads the idiot. 'I'll buy you another drachma with my own money!'

Friend: Three nights ago, I saw you in my dream.
Idiot: Liar! I was in the countryside.

A young idiot is playing around at home, pretending to be a gladiator. Suddenly someone shouts that his father is coming home, so he quickly throws down the armour and unties the shin pads. Before he knows it, his father is standing in the room, so the idiot grabs his book and starts reading – not realizing he's still wearing a helmet.

An idiot asks a ship's captain what time it is. When the captain says he doesn't know, the idiot asks him how long he has been the captain of that ship. The captain tells him it's been three years.

'I don't get it,' says the idiot. 'I only bought my house six months ago, and I can already guess the time pretty well based on when the sun comes over into the courtyard. How come you can't tell the exact time based on when the sun comes over onto this boat you've had for so long?'

AN IDIOT WENT TO HIS SCHOOL FRIENDS' PLACE FOR DINNER, WHERE EVERYONE RAVED ABOUT THE PIG'S HEAD THAT WAS SERVED. THE NEXT DAY, IT WAS THE IDIOT'S TURN TO HOST, SO HE WENT TO THE BUTCHER AND SAID, 'GIVE ME ANOTHER HEAD OF THAT SAME PIG – IT WAS ABSOLUTELY DELICIOUS YESTERDAY.'

IDIOTS

An idiot who thought he was good at giving eulogies wrote one for a man who was still alive. The guy called him on this – and the idiot's reply was, 'Well, you can't predict when you'll die. When the time comes, I don't want to get the eulogy wrong and look like an idiot.'

The same idiot again: 'Father, how much wine does a five-cup jug hold?'

This time his friend has bought a ladder. The idiot asks him, 'I know it has twenty steps going up – but how many has it got on the way down?'

Some guys are discussing their terrible indigestion, and the idiot says he's never had it.

'So you never spew out anything gross?' they ask.

'Oh, yes,' replies the idiot. 'Every day.'

An idiot has a baby boy and people ask what he is called.

'I will give him my name,' says the idiot. 'But I will still be me.'

An idiot whose wife has died is buying a coffin, and gets into a fight about how much it's worth. The salesman swears on his life that he won't sell it for less than 50,000 drachmas.

'Fine,' says the idiot. 'Since you've made a solemn oath, take the 50,000 – but throw in a child's coffin so that I have it to hand when my son dies.'

TWO COWARDLY IDIOTS ARE BEING CHASED BY SOLDIERS, SO ONE HIDES IN A WELL AND THE OTHER HIDES IN SOME REEDS. THE SOLDIERS STOP BY THE WELL AND LOWER A HELMET TO GET SOME WATER, AND, THINKING A SOLDIER IS CLIMBING DOWN, THE IDIOT IN THE WELL IMMEDIATELY SURRENDERS.

SURPRISED, THE SOLDIERS TELL HIM THAT THEY WOULD HAVE PASSED HIM BY HAD HE KEPT QUIET – AT WHICH POINT THE IDIOT IN THE REEDS PIPES UP: 'WELL, PASS ME BY, THEN – I'VE KEPT QUIET!'

FRIEND: CAN I BORROW A CLOAK – JUST TO GO DOWN TO THE COUNTRYSIDE?
IDIOT: SORRY, I'VE ONLY GOT ONE THAT GOES DOWN TO THE ANKLE.

IDIOTS

Friend: Congratulations on the birth of your son!
Idiot: Thanks – I hope one day your friends can do the same for you!

An idiot is staring at two twins, amazed at their similarity.

'You know,' he says, 'this one looks much more similar to his brother than his brother does to him.'

An idiot is being driven in a cart, when the mules become exhausted and can't move another inch. The driver unties them so they can rest a bit – but as soon as he does so, they peg it. The idiot turns to the driver and yells, 'You see? The mules are running fine – the cart was the reason we weren't moving!'

MISERS

Did you hear the one about the miser who was writing his will? He appointed himself as the heir.

A swindler is always conning his girlfriend into believing he's posh and has loads of money. One day, when he's eating at his neighbour's house, he suddenly sees his girlfriend.

'I say!' he says loudly, turning in her direction. 'Will you fetch me my ornate cape at once?'

A miser is asked why he never eats anything but olives.

'Simple,' he replies. 'The olive's flesh serves as a meal, the stone as firewood, and when I've eaten, I can wash my whole head with the oil and not need a bath.'

Another guy like him – a big boaster with no money – gets really sick. His girlfriend calls round unexpectedly to find him sleeping on a mat. Suddenly embarrassed, he says, 'Ah, the very finest and most expensive doctors of the city have ordered me to sleep on this mat.'

In the market, a pompous man sees his boy servant, who's just come in from the countryside.

'How are my sheep doing?' he asks.

'One of them is sleeping,' says the boy, 'and the other one is up and about.'

ABDERITES

Abdera was a city-state in Thrace (northeastern Greece). Following – and indeed because of – its illustrious beginnings around the sixth century BC, Abdera was repeatedly besieged and overrun by all manner of marauding armies, and it is perhaps as a result of all this besieging and overrunning that the Abderites were deemed to be totally incompetent and entirely stupid. Whether they actually were stupid is not a matter with which people concerned themselves.

After all, who doesn't enjoy a spot of casual xenophobia?

Abdera is divided into two, with some people living in the east and others in the west. When the city was suddenly attacked, the ones in the east said to each other, 'No need to worry – the enemy have only come in through the western gate.'

In Abdera, a donkey escapes and runs into a gymnasium, knocking over all the oil. The Abderites round up all the city's donkeys and herd them into one place, where they whip the naughty donkey in front of all the others as a warning.

An Abderite is trying to hang himself, when the rope snaps and he hits his head. He goes to the doctor, gets some cream to treat his injury – and then goes home again and hangs himself.

An Abderite meets a eunuch and asks how many kids he has. The eunuch tells him he doesn't have the testicles to be able to produce children.

'I see,' says the Abderite. 'Well, I hope at least that you have many grandchildren.'

An Abderite meets a eunuch who's chatting with a woman, and asks him if this is his wife. When he's told that eunuchs can't have wives, the Abderite says, 'My mistake – it must be your daughter.'

An Abderite is out for a walk, and sees a guy with a massive hernia going for a piss at the side of the street. He mutters to his friend, 'Looks like he'll be emptying himself until midnight!'

DID YOU HEAR ABOUT THE
ABDERITE WHO WAS TOLD THAT
ONIONS AND CABBAGE CAUSE
WIND? HE TOOK A SACK OF THE
VEGETABLES OUT SAILING WITH
HIM ON A CALM DAY, AND HUNG
THEM FROM THE STERN.

An Abderite sees a eunuch coming out of the public bath with a bulging hernia. He turns to his friend and whispers, 'I see it's not just the baths that have things pouring out of them!'

An Abderite is sleeping in the same bed as a guy with a hernia. He gets up in the middle of the night to use the bathroom, and when he comes back, it's pitch black and he accidentally steps on the hernia. His friend screams out in pain, and the Abderite asks, 'Why on earth are you sleeping with your head down on this side?'

An Abderite sees a guy with a hernia climbing out of the bath, barely able to stand upright, and asks, 'Why have you filled yourself up with so much booze that you can't carry yourself decently?'

An Abderite sees an athlete who has been hung up on
a cross.

'Good heavens!' he exclaims. 'He's not running anymore
– he's flying!'

An Abderite is dreaming that he's selling a pig, and
is asking 100 drachmas for it. One guy offers him 50
drachmas, but the Abderite refuses. At that moment, he
wakes up – so quickly shuts his eyes again and sticks out
his hand, saying, 'OK, give me the 50, then.'

Q: What did the Abderite eunuch get for his birthday?
A: A hernia.

An Abderite owes someone a donkey, but doesn't have one.
So he asks the guy if he can repay his debt in two instalments.

AN ABDERITE IS SELLING A POT
WHOSE EAR-SHAPED HANDLES
ARE MISSING. WHEN ASKED WHY
THEY'RE MISSING, HE REPLIES, 'SO
THAT IT DOESN'T HEAR THAT IT'S
BEING SOLD, AND RUN AWAY.'

AN ABDERITE HAS JUST BEEN
TO HIS FATHER'S CREMATION
CEREMONY, AND RUNS HOME
TO HIS SICK MOTHER.

'THERE'S STILL A BIT OF WOOD
LEFT ON THE FIRE,' HE TELLS HER.
'IF YOU LIKE, YOU CAN CREMATE
YOURSELF, TOO.'

AN ABDERITE'S SPARROW DIES.
A FEW MONTHS LATER, HE SEES
AN OSTRICH AND LAMENTS,
'IF MY LITTLE BIRD WERE STILL
ALIVE, HE WOULD HAVE GROWN
TO BE THAT BIG.'

SIDONIANS

The ancient settlement of Sidon was one of the largest cities in Phoenicia, and still exists in modern-day Lebanon.

Sidon was quite the centre of industry, famous for manufacturing glass and a highly desirable purple dye – they were simpler times – and, according to the Bible, even Jesus paid the place a visit.

But, alas, the Sidonians suffered from the same problem as the Abderites – they were foreign – and they were thus written off as a bunch of total morons.

A Sidonian lawyer is chatting with two friends. One says that it's not right to slaughter sheep because they give us milk and wool. The other says that it's not right to kill cows because they give us milk and pull our ploughs. Then the lawyer adds that it's not right to kill pigs either, because they give us liver, bacon and pork chops.

A Sidonian doctor's patient dies, and he receives 1,000 drachmas in the will as gratitude for looking after him in his sickness. As he's following the body in the funeral procession, he starts grumbling about how little money he was left.

A year later, the dead guy's son falls ill, and he calls the doctor to come and treat his illness. 'If you leave me 5,000 drachmas in your will,' says the doctor, 'I'll treat you the same as I did your father.'

A Sidonian centurion sees someone driving his cart
through the marketplace, which isn't allowed, so he orders
him to be beaten.

'But I'm a Roman,' protests the man, 'and it's against
the law to beat me.'

So the centurion orders the horses to be whipped
at once.

Sidonian student: How much does a five-cup jug hold?
Teacher: Is it wine or oil?

Someone asks a Sidonian cook, 'Can I borrow one of your
knives as far as Smyrna?'

'Sorry,' says the cook, 'I don't have one that long.'

Someone says to a Sidonian fisherman, 'Look – you've only been able to catch crabs in your lobster pot.'

'Unlike you,' replies the Sidonian. '*You've* caught crabs all over your body!'

Smart-Arses

A smart-arse sees a dumb professor trying to teach literature, and suggests that he should teach the lyre instead.

'But I have no idea how to play the lyre,' the professor protests.

'The same goes for teaching literature,' says the smart-arse.

A smart-arse wrestler falls down into the mud. Not wanting to look like a failure, he rolls around in it, and then stands up and flexes his muscles.

A crook doctor visits a patient with bad conjunctivitis, and, having asked to borrow a lamp, he decides not to return it. On one visit, he asks his patient how his eyes are doing.

'Well,' answers the smart-arse, 'since the day you borrowed my lamp, I haven't been able to see it.'

A smart-arse has been insulted in the bathhouse, so he goes to court and calls the bath attendants as witnesses. When the defence lawyer dismisses them as unreliable witnesses, the smart-arse waxes lyrical.

'In the days of yore,' he says, 'were I to be insulted inside the Horse of Troy, I would have called as witnesses such great people as Menelaus, and Odysseus, and Diomedes ...

'But since this happened in the bathhouse,' he continues, 'this lot will have to do.'

A SMART-ARSE SEES A SLOW
RUNNER, AND SAYS, 'I KNOW
WHAT THAT GUY NEEDS
TO CATCH UP WITH
HIS COMPETITORS.'

THE COACH ASKS HIM WHAT
THAT MIGHT BE.

'A HORSE.'

A smart-arse sees a brothel-owner pimping out a prostitute with skin as black as the night, and asks him, 'How much do you charge for the night?'

Patient: Doctor, doctor, I'm covered in red-hot boils and I'm burning up.
Doctor: Get yourself a kettle – you'll have warm water for days!

Sailor: Where's the wind coming from today?
Captain: Onions and cabbages.

A smart-arse steals a pig and runs off with it. When he's caught, he drops the pig onto the ground and smacks it, saying, 'Dig up the ground there – don't come back on my land!'

Two blokes come up out of the public bath and ask the smart-arse if they can borrow his towel. He's never met one of them before, and he recognizes the other as a thief.

'I can't lend it to you,' he tells the first, 'because I don't know you.'

He turns to the second man.

'And I can't lend it to *you*,' he says, 'because I *do* know you.'

A smart-arse comes across a singer who's out of tune and making terrible racket, and shouts, 'Cockerel!'

The performer asks him why he's calling him that.

'Because as soon as you start crowing,' the wit explains, 'everyone gets up.'

HAIRDRESSER: HOW SHALL I CUT YOUR HAIR, SIR?
CLIENT: IN SILENCE.

Smart-Arses

A smart-arse street vendor comes across a soldier on top
of his wife. He says, 'This is not the sort of transaction I
was after!'

KYMAEANS

K yme (now Kymi on the island of Euboea) was a coastal city in Greece.

From the eighth century BC, the Kymaeans began venturing across seas to establish colonies, notably in southern Italy. They brought with them the so-called Cumaean alphabet – Kyme's variation on the standard Greek alphabet of the time – which gradually gave rise to the Latin or Roman alphabet we use today.

Nonetheless, Kyme was a bit foreign, so it naturally follows that the Kymaeans were total imbeciles.

A KYMAEAN TAKES HIS FATHER'S
BODY TO ALEXANDRIA TO BE
EMBALMED. WHEN HE GOES BACK
TO PICK HIM UP, THE EMBALMER
HAS SEVERAL BODIES READY FOR
COLLECTION SO ASKS HOW HE
MIGHT RECOGNIZE THE FATHER.

'HE HAD A COUGH.'

A Kymaean prepares a massive area for separating his grain. He stands on one side of it and shouts across to his wife, 'Hey! Can you see me?'

'Only just!' she yells back.

'When the right season comes around,' shouts the husband, 'I'll prepare the area so big that you won't see me at all!'

A Kymaean goes to visit a friend and stands outside his house shouting for him. A neighbour sticks his head out of the window and says, 'Shout louder – then he'll hear you.'

So the Kymaean yells out, 'Hey! Louder!'

Did you hear the one about the Kymaean thief who went to steal from a moneylender's house? He stole the longest-looking invoice he could find.

A Kymaean sees a sheep being sheared with its feet tied together and says, 'Thank god my master doesn't do the same to me when he cuts my hair!'

Did you hear the one about the Kymaean who bought stolen clothes? He covered them in tar so that no one would recognize them.

The Kymaeans are expecting a revered guest to return from overseas. They want to honour him with clean water in the public baths, but they only have one pool. So they fill it with fresh warm water and position a grate across the middle, so that at least half the water stays clean for their guest.

A KYMAEAN IS SELLING SOME HONEY. A FRIEND TRIES IT AND SAYS IT'S ABSOLUTELY DELICIOUS.

'I KNOW,' SAYS THE KYMAEAN. 'AND I'D KEEP IT FOR MYSELF IF ONLY THAT MOUSE HADN'T FALLEN INTO IT.'

CHANGING
ROOMS

A Kymaean is riding past a garden on his donkey and notices a branch laden with ripe figs hanging right above him. He grabs hold of the branch – but his donkey runs away from under him, leaving him hanging in the tree.

A passing gardener asks him what on earth he's doing all the way up there, and the Kymaean replies, 'I fell off my donkey.'

A doctor gives up on a Kymaean patient, saying he's too sick to save. The patient makes a miraculous recovery, however, and takes to avoiding the doctor whenever he sees him. Eventually the doctor asks why he's ignoring him.

'You said I would die,' says the Kymaean, 'and I'm embarrassed to prove you wrong.'

While his father is out of town, a Kymaean is convicted of a serious crime and sentenced to death. As he walks out of the court, he shouts out, 'Whatever you do, please don't tell my dad – he'll absolutely kill me!'

A man accuses that same Kymaean of robbing him.

'Well, if I did,' replies the Kymaean, 'may I never return from wherever I'm heading now.'

A Kymaean doctor is treating an extremely sick patient, and orders him to be given an enema so as to examine what comes out. When he is later told that the patient has died, he responds, 'Well, I swear he would have burst had we not given him that enema.'

A KYMAEAN SURGEON IS SEWING STITCHES INTO A PATIENT'S HEAD WOUND. HE FLIPS THE PATIENT ONTO HIS BACK AND POURS WATER INTO HIS MOUTH – TO SEE IF HIS HANDIWORK HAS STOPPED IT FROM LEAKING OUT.

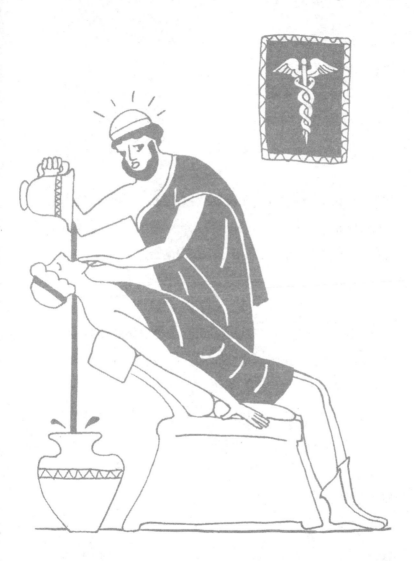

A guy asks a Kymaean shopkeeper where the lawyer Dracontides lives.

'I'm all alone here,' the Kymaean replies. 'But if you watch my shop, I'll come with you and show you.'

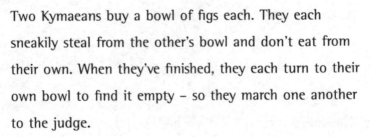

Did you hear the one about the Kymaean doctor who brought a patient from second-stage fever down to first-stage fever? He only charged half the fee.

Two Kymaeans buy a bowl of figs each. They each sneakily steal from the other's bowl and don't eat from their own. When they've finished, they each turn to their own bowl to find it empty – so they march one another to the judge.

He orders the men to refund the emptied bowls with their emptied bowels.

In the Kymaean assembly, a politician is accused of a crime.

'Fellow citizens,' he protests, 'the people who have made these false allegations against me are just slanderers. I swear – if I've committed these crimes, let this whole auditorium crumble on top of me as you sit here and watch!'

A Kymaean judge was known for making proclamations like this:

- 'As soon as the sacrifice is over, the officials must present their own hides to the priest.'
- 'The councillors must go into the council chamber, but mustn't hold council.'
- 'The cooks must throw their own bones over the city walls.'
- 'The shoe-makers mustn't have shoe-moulds that are too small.'

At a dignitary's funeral in Kyme, someone goes up to the officials and asks, 'Who's the dead guy?'

One of the Kymaeans turns around and points.

'The one lying in the coffin.'

Did you hear the one about the Kymaean who was trying to sell his house? He carried around one of the bricks to show people what it was like.

The Kymaeans are rebuilding their city walls, and a guy named Lollianus rebuilds two whole sections out of his own pocket. The other citizens, feeling envious, become angry at him for doing this, so when the city comes under attack, they decree that those sections of the wall should be defended by Lollianus alone.

Did you hear about the Kymaean surgeon whose patient started screaming in pain? He decided to use a blunter scalpel.

A Kymaean is swimming in the sea when it starts to rain – so he dives underwater to avoid getting wet.

Did you hear the one about the Kymaean shopping for windows? He asked if there were any that faced south.

Some Kymaeans go along to vote. They realize that loads of people from other cities haven't turned up, and they blame the condition of the roads.

'We'd be total idiots,' they say, 'if we even bothered coming ourselves next time.'

OBSTINATE BASTARDS

A guy tells an obstinate senator, 'I'd like to see you in your office for a short time.'

The senator replies, 'And I'd like to see you blind and lame.'

Patient: Doctor, doctor – I've been passing blood and gall when I go to the toilet.

Doctor: I wouldn't care if you had the gall to shit out your whole insides.

An obstinate one-eyed doctor asks a patient how he's doing.

'I'm as you see me,' the patient says.

'Oh,' replies the doctor. 'In that case, I'm sorry to say that one half of you has died.'

An obstinate bastard is selling a jug of honey in the market. When someone asks him how much he's selling it for, he turns the jug upside down and says, 'I'll pour out my own blood like this before I tell you!'

An obstinate astrologer is reading the future of a sick child. He assures the mother that the child will live for a long time, and asks for his fee. When she tells him to come and collect it tomorrow, he says, 'But what if the boy dies overnight? Will I still get paid?'

Someone asks an obstinate bastard where he lives.

'I'm moving house,' he replies.

Ⓢ

A man goes to his obstinate friend's house looking
for him.

'I'm not in!' comes the shout from inside.

Laughing, the friend says, 'Liar! I recognize your voice!'

'You bastard!' replies the obstinate guy. 'If my slave had
called out, you would have believed him – how come you
trust him more than me?'

Ⓢ

A doctor says to his patient, 'You've got a really bad fever.'

'Well, if you think you can have a better fever,' the
patient retorts, 'lie down on that bed and go for it.'

Ⓢ

An obstinate bastard is walking down the stairs when he trips and falls. The housekeeper shouts out, 'Who's fallen?'

The reply from the bottom of the stairs: 'I should be able to make noise in my own home if I so choose!'

Patient: Doctor, doctor – I can't lie down, stand up, or sit down.
Doctor: Try hanging.

A doctor is treating an obstinate patient, and orders him to copy the sparrow and only eat small amounts.

'If I have to copy the sparrow,' says the patient, 'how on earth am I supposed to climb into a birdcage?'

An obstinate bastard is sitting down playing a game of dice, when an unemployed man comes over and starts giving his opinions on the game. The obstinate guy asks him what his profession is and why he's unemployed.

'I'm a tailor,' says the man, 'but I haven't got any work at the moment.'

So the dice player tears a hole in his cloak and hands it over, saying, 'Take this work and shut up.'

APPRENTICES

A young student asks an apprentice teacher, 'How are you supposed to say it: "two of them" or "double"?'

So the teacher sticks up his hand and shows two fingers.

Student: What's Priam's mother called?

Apprentice teacher: Er ... Well, out of respect, I think we should call her 'madam'.

AN APPRENTICE HAIRDRESSER
WAS ALWAYS INJURING HIS
CLIENTS, AND SO HE CARRIED
AROUND PLASTERS TO TREAT
THEM AS AND WHEN. ONE DAY,
A CLIENT COMPLAINED ABOUT
HIS INJURY.

'WHAT ARE YOU COMPLAINING
FOR?' PROTESTED THE
HAIRDRESSER. 'YOU'VE ONLY PAID
ONE DRACHMA FOR YOUR SHAVE,
BUT YOU'RE GETTING
FOUR DRACHMAS' WORTH
OF MEDICAL TREATMENT!'

121

AN APPRENTICE IS ORDERED BY
HIS BOSS TO GIVE A MANICURE
TO THE LADY OF THE HOUSE,
BUT HE STARTS CRYING AS SOON
AS HE ARRIVES. SHE ASKS HIM
WHAT'S WRONG.

'DON'T WORRY, I'M BEING SILLY,'
WAILS THE APPRENTICE. 'IT'S JUST
THAT I KNOW I'M GOING TO CUT
YOUR FINGERS, AND I'M SCARED
MY BOSS WILL BEAT ME.'

A man has just come back from overseas and goes to an apprentice psychic to ask after his family.

'They're all well,' declares the psychic, 'including your father.'

'But my father's been dead for ten years!' the man retorts.

'Ah,' says the psychic. 'Well, in that case, you clearly don't know who your real father is.'

A man asks an apprentice astrologer if his enemy will ever return from abroad, and the astrologer assures him that he won't. But the next day the guy finds out his enemy is back.

'I know!' says the astrologer. 'He has absolutely no shame!'

An apprentice is giving a client a terrible manicure and accidentally cuts his finger. When the client refuses to let him continue, the apprentice turns around and says, 'Boss – you really should have had me trained before I treated clients.'

An apprentice astrologer is babbling away and tells someone, 'It is not in your stars to ever have children.'

'But I've got seven kids!' says the man.

'Oh,' replies the astronomer. 'Well, you'd better look after them, then.'

An apprentice astrologer is captured by enemy soldiers. As they're preparing to go into battle, he tells them, 'You will win the battle. But if they are able to pluck the hairs from the back of your necks as you stand in the battle line – well, then you probably won't.'

COWARDS

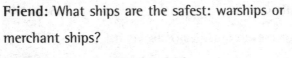

Friend: What ships are the safest: warships or merchant ships?

Coward: The ones in dry dock.

A man asks a cowardly boxer, 'Whom are you fighting today?'

The boxer points out his opponent and says, 'The winner over there.'

Another cowardly boxer writes on his forehead: 'Fragile: contains vital organs.' But his opponent keeps on striking him.

'Can't you read?' yells the coward. 'How come you're still killing me?'

The same boxer is being struck by his opponent over and over again.

'Please!' he shouts out. 'Don't all hit me at once!'

Two cowards are sleeping in the same bed. A thief comes in and steals the blanket from them.

'Go and catch him,' says one to the other.

'Don't worry,' replies his friend, 'we'll get him when he comes back to steal our pillows.'

DID YOU HEAR THE ONE ABOUT
THE COWARDLY HUNTER WHO
WAS CHASED BY BEARS IN HIS
SLEEP? HE BOUGHT SOME DOGS
AND HAD THEM SLEEP BESIDE HIM.

COWARDS

A coward is owed one drachma by another coward. They bump into each other and the first coward asks the second for his drachma.

'Reach out and take it from my pocket,' he replies.

'Oh, don't worry,' says the first coward. 'Let's just call it quits.'

ENVIOUS PEOPLE

A cloth-maker uses urine to treat his wares, and a man goes along to donate some. But he's the only donor who isn't able to piss, so he kills himself.

An envious landlord sees that his tenants are really happy. So he evicts them.

An envious guy sees his neighbour putting up a good fight against wild animals at the games. He leans over to the official and whispers, 'Bring out the bear.'

FAT PEOPLE

One fat guy is giving his daughter's hand in marriage to another, and is asked what the dowry is.

'I'm giving you a house,' he replies, 'which looks out over the bakery.'

A fat gym teacher spies a loaf of bread hanging from the ceiling.

'Hey!' he shouts at it. 'Are you coming down? What do you say? Or do I need to come up there and finish you off?'

A fat guy is invited to the harvest by his friend, and absolutely stuffs himself with figs and grapes before falling asleep. Because of his upset stomach, he dreams that he sees his friend sitting in a fig tree, calling him over to climb up and eat with him. As they sit up in the tree, they have a laugh shitting down from the branches.

Overcome by the vivid dream, the fat guy shits all over his bed sheets. He wakes up and washes the sheets, and, after another snack of figs, goes back to sleep.

Once again he dreams that his friend is sitting up in the tree and beckoning him over in the same way.

'You want to embarrass me again!' he calls to his friend. 'You want me to think I'm up in a tree and then shit all over the bed sheets again. But I won't be fooled this time – I'll go for a shit first, and then climb up the tree!'

With that, he promptly shits himself again.

A FAT ACTOR ASKS HIS DIRECTOR IF HE CAN EAT BREAKFAST BEFORE HE GOES ON STAGE. WHEN ASKED WHY, THE ACTOR REPLIES, 'SO THAT I'M NOT MAKING A FALSE OATH WHEN I READ MY LINE: "I SWEAR BY ARTEMIS THAT I HAVE HAD THE MOST DELIGHTFUL BREAKFAST."'

A fat guy offers a gardener four drachmas in return for all the figs he can eat. The gardener rolls his eyes, and says, 'OK – you can have as many as you like from these trees here.' So the fat guy climbs to very top of the biggest trees and starts eating every single fig in sight.

After a few hours, the gardener suddenly remembers the guy, so goes looking for him. Finding him at the top of one tree, shaking the branches and stuffing his face, the gardener gets angry.

'Couldn't you have stayed down here and eaten from the branches that are hanging over the path?' he shouts.

'Give me time,' yells the fat man. 'I'm working my way down to those ones.'

A fat guy spots a loaf of bread lying on top of a
doorframe.

'Oh gods, I beg you,' he starts, 'either make me taller,
or the door shorter.'

The same fat guy then goes to the baker and offers him
two drachmas for all the bread he can eat. Thinking that
one loaf will suffice, the baker takes the money, and the
fat guy starts eating. Shocked to see the man devour half
a basket of loaves while still standing, the baker asks,
'Why don't you sit down here and eat?'

'I want to finish off this basket first,' says the customer,
'and then I'll sit down and eat the loaves on the counter.'

Did you hear about the fat doctor who saw a loaf
of bread stuck in a hole? He treated it with an
antiseptic salve.

A doctor is examining a fat patient. He orders him to stick
to a diet of wheat in water, or oats in water if he can't
find wheat. Misunderstanding him, the glutton says, 'Fine
– and if I can't find any goats, I'll just eat two kids.'

DRUNKS

A drunk is sitting in a bar when someone rushes up to him and says, 'Your wife is dead.'

The drunk leans over bar and says, 'In that case, barman, I think you'd better pour me a drink.'

A drunk inherited a vineyard – but the harvest season killed him.

Did you hear the one about the drunk who opened a bar? He tied a bear up outside.

A DRUNK WAS BEING TOLD OFF BY A FRIEND FOR HAVING LOST HIS SENSES BECAUSE OF THE BOOZE.

'WHO'S CONFUSED THEIR SENSES?' SLURRED THE ALCOHOLIC. 'ME – OR YOU WITH YOUR TWO HEADS?'

BAD BREATH
AND FARTING

A young guy sits down in the theatre between two men –
one with bad breath and the other with bad body odour.
Noticing a bad smell, he turns to one of the men and
asks, 'Who farted?'

Suddenly aware that the smell is coming from the
man's mouth, he turns to the other man and speaks
into his ear.

Suddenly aware of the second smell, he gets up
and leaves.

A guy with bad breath decides it's time to commit suicide
– so he wraps up his head, and exhales.

A guy with bad breath bumps into a deaf guy and says,
'Hi there!'

'Eurgh!' exclaims the deaf guy.

'What did I say?' asks the man.

'Sorry, I thought you farted.'

A guy with bad breath goes to see his doctor and says,
'Doctor, doctor – look how my tonsils have swollen
and dropped.'

As soon as he opens his mouth, the doctor recoils.

'The problem is not that your tonsils have dropped,' he
says, 'but that your arse has risen.'

A GUY WITH BAD BREATH
IS KISSING HIS WIFE AND
WHISPERING, 'OH, MY GODDESS,
MY APHRODITE ...'

SHE TURNS AWAY AND SAYS,
'OH MY GOD ...'

A GUY WITH BAD BREATH IS
ALWAYS LOOKING UP TO THE
HEAVENS AND PRAYING.

'DO ME A FAVOUR,' CALLS DOWN
ZEUS, TURNING HIS FACE AWAY.
'PRAY TO THE GODS IN THE
UNDERWORLD!'

A guy with bad breath is cuddling his young child, and then chews up some food to feed to him.

The child turns away and says, 'Daddy, I don't eat shit.'

A guy with bad breath asks his wife, 'Darling, why do you hate me?'

'Because you kiss me,' she replies.

An idiot, who is sleeping in the same room as a deaf guy, farts in the night. When the smell wafts over, the deaf guy makes a noise of disgust.

'So you *can* hear!' the idiot cries.

HORNY WOMEN AND LONG-SUFFERING HUSBANDS

A young actor was loved by two women – one with bad breath, and the other with bad body odour.

'Darling, kiss me!' said one and 'Darling, hold me!' implored the other.

The actor read from his script: '"Oh gods, what am I to do? I am split between two evils!"'

A young man says to his wife, 'Darling, what do you want to do? Eat breakfast or have sex?'

'Whatever you want,' she replies. 'But we're out of food.'

A young man invites two lecherous old hags to his house, and asks his housekeeper to serve them.

'Prepare a drink for one of them,' he orders, 'and have sex with the other if she wants it.'

'We don't drink,' say the women in unison.

A misogynist is standing in the middle of the market place shouting, 'Wife for sale! Tax-free!'

When asked why he's selling her, he replies, 'So that she misses me.'

At a woman's funeral, a stranger solemnly asks, 'Who is resting here?'

'I am!' cries the widower, '... Now that she's gone.'

A man is really sick and on his last legs.

'If anything happens to you,' his wife says, 'I'll hang myself.'

The husband looks up at her and replies, 'Do it while I'm still alive, darling.'

One guy had a nagging, abusive wife. When she died, he carried her body out on a shield. A passer-by asked why.

'She liked a battle,' he replied.

A young man asks his friend whether his wife bosses him around, or if she obeys his every word. Trying to show off, the young man replies, 'She's so scared of me that every time I open my mouth, she shits herself.'

ODDS AND ENDS

The lady of a house notices that her idiot servant has an exceptionally large dick, and she becomes obsessed with him. She puts on a mask so that he won't recognize her and then starts fooling around with him – needless to remark, he has a good time with her, too.

Later that day, the servant meets the master of the house.

'Master, master!' he says. 'I shagged the dancer – but when I entered her, it was your wife on the inside!'

AN IDIOT IS SAILING INTO A
STORM. ALL THE PASSENGERS
GRAB HOLD OF THINGS THAT WILL
HELP SAVE THEM, SO THE IDIOT
GRABS HOLD OF THE ANCHOR.

An idiot buys some meat. As he's carrying it home, a hawk swoops down and snatches it from his hands.

'Let me become just like you,' shouts the idiot, 'if I don't do the same to someone else!'

An idiot hears that a crow can live for up to 200 years, so he buys one to see if it's true.

An idiot teacher hears that one of his students is sick. Later he hears that the boy has a fever, and the next day he's told by the father that the boy has died.

'You can come up with any excuse you like,' the teacher retorts, 'but it's your son's education that will suffer.'

A smart-arse goes abroad, where he gets a hernia. When he returns, a friend asks what he's brought back with him.

'For you, nothing,' says the smart-arse. 'But for my thighs I've brought a pillow.'

A greedy magistrate demands that his court be held next to the bakery.

A guy is teasing his friend and says, 'I screwed your wife last night.'

'As her husband, I *have* to do it,' says the husband. 'What's your excuse?'

A smart-arse lawyer is prosecuting a senator who starts dozing off in court.

'Objection!' screams the lawyer.

'To what?' asks the senator.

'To you falling asleep!' comes the reply.

FURTHER READING

Berg, William (trans.), *Philogelos: The Laugh Addict*
(yudu.com, 2008)

Boissonade, Jean François (ed.), G. *Pachymeris,*
'Declamationes XIII', Hieroclis et Philagrii
Grammaticorum: Philogelos (Dumont/Leleux, 1848)

Eberhard, Alfred (ed.), *Philogelos: Hieroclis et Philagrii*
Facetiae (H. Ebeling & C. Plahn, 1869)

Holt, Jim, *Stop Me If You've Heard This: A History and*
Philosophy of Jokes (Profile Books, 2008)